CIRCULATING WITH THE LISTED PROBLEM(S):

Back of Book bent

7 3   3-13

DO NOT REMOVE
CARDS FROM POCKET

COWS

FARM ANIMAL DISCOVERY LIBRARY

Lynn M. Stone

Rourke Corporation, Inc.
Vero Beach, Florida 32964

PHOTO CREDITS

All photos by the author

ACKNOWLEDGEMENTS

The author thanks the following for assistance in the
preparation of photos for this book: Carol Boesche, DeKalb, Ill.;
Herb Ruh, Big Rock, Ill.; Bob Gehrke, Elgin, Ill.

LIBRARY OF CONGRESS
Library of Congress Cataloging-in-Publication Data
Stone, Lynn M.
　Cows / by Lynn M. Stone.

　　p.　cm. — (Farm animal discovery library)
　　Summary: An introduction to the physical characteristics,
habits, and natural environment of cows and their
relationship to humans.
　　ISBN 0-86593-039-2
　　1. Cattle—Juvenile literature. 2. Cows—Juvenile literature.
[1. Cows.] I. Title. II. Series: Stone, Lynn M. Farm animal
discovery library.
SF197.5.S76　1990
636.2—dc20　　　　　　　89-29869
　　　　　　　　　　　　　　　　CIP
　　　　　　　　　　　　　　　　AC

TABLE OF CONTENTS

COWS

Cows *(Bos taurus)* are large, heavy farm animals. They are important for their meat and **dairy** products—milk, butter, and cheese.

Cows are also known as cattle. The word "cow" is sometimes used to mean female cattle which have had a baby, or calf.

There were no cattle in North America until they were imported from other countries.

Explorers from northern Europe may have brought cattle to North America a thousand years ago. The Spanish brought cattle to North America in the early 1500's.

Illinois dairy farm

HOW COWS LOOK

Many cows have horns. Farmers often remove horns so that a cow can not injure the farmer or other cows.

Some types of cattle do not grow horns. They are called **polled** cattle.

Female cattle raised for milking have large **udders.** These are bags underneath the cows which contain milk.

Cattle may weigh from about 700 pounds to more than 2,000 pounds. The largest cattle are the **bulls,** or adult males.

Holstein cow

WHERE COWS LIVE

Domestic animals are the kinds of tame animals that have been raised by people for many years. Domestic cows have been raised for about 8,000 years in some parts of the world.

Cows are now raised almost everywhere there are people. They live in cold places like Iceland and Alaska. They are also raised in warm countries such as Kenya and India.

The United States has about 110 million cattle. India has over 180 million cattle, more than any other country.

Brahma bull in Florida

BREEDS OF COWS

Thousands of years ago, all cattle were wild animals. One type was the aurochs, which lived in Europe. A few aurochs were caught and tamed, or domesticated.

Over hundreds of years the aurochs were mated with other kinds of cattle. Cattle somewhat different from the aurochs began to appear. These new types of cattle formed new **breeds.**

The most popular dairy breeds in North America are the Holstein, Jersey, Guernsey, Ayrshire, and Brown Swiss. The Angus, Brahman, Charolais, Hereford, and Simmental are popular **beef** breeds.

Hereford cow

Guernsey chewing cud

Cattle in Swiss Alps

WILD COWS

The last aurochs cattle disappeared in the 1620's. But many other cattle still live in the wild.

Wild cattle are closely related to domestic cows, which scientists call *Bos taurus.* The banteng, guar, and kouprey are wild cattle of warm Asian countries. The shaggy yak lives in the mountains of Tibet.

Other hoofed animals that are cousins of cattle are antelope, bison, buffalo, goats, and sheep.

The yak, a wild cow

BABY COWS

A young female cow, called a **heifer,** usually has her first calf when she is two years old. For several years afterward, she will have one calf per year. (Sometimes she will have twins.)

Most female dairy calves are raised to adulthood. Cows may live to be 20.

Male calves are sometimes sold for meat known as veal. Some bull calves have an operation and are raised as **steers.** Steers cannot mate with cows and have calves of their own.

Guernsey calf and cow

HOW COWS ARE RAISED

Cattle eat grass, hay, corn, and soybean meal. Sometimes they graze in pastures. At other times they are fed directly by farmers.

In the American West, herds of beef cattle wander over huge areas of open land. They graze on grass. They are rounded up, often by cowboys on horseback, at market time.

Dairy cattle graze in smaller pastures. They enter a barn each morning and evening to be milked.

During winter, dairy cows remain in or close to the barn.

*Brown Swiss cow
in Switzerland*

HOW COWS ACT

Cows are not very active animals. They rarely move fast. Most of their time is spent grazing or resting.

A cow chews a **cud.** Cows swallow their meal, then bring it up from their stomach for a second chewing. The food brought up is called the cud.

Female cattle are usually gentle. Bulls are often short-tempered and very dangerous.

The ring in a bull's nose helps the farmer control the animal. A sharp tug on a chain attached to the ring hurts the bull's nose.

Holstein bull

HOW COWS ARE USED

Dairy cattle are valued for their milk. An average dairy cow produces about 1500 gallons (6000 quarts) of milk each year.

Holstein cows produce more milk than other breeds. Breeds such as Guernseys and Jerseys produce richer milk.

Beef cattle are raised for their meat. They tend to have thicker bodies and shorter legs than dairy cattle.

Cattle hides are used for shoes, belts, wallets, jackets, and other leather goods.

Yaks in Tibet are raised for milk, meat, skin, and their wooly hair. Yaks pull carts, too.

Glossary

beef (BEEF)—the meat of cattle; a type of cattle raised for meat

breed (BREED)—closely related group of animals that came about through man's help; a type of domestic cattle

bull (BULL)—male cattle

cud (CUHD)—food which is being chewed after already having been swallowed once

dairy (DARE ee)—milk products, or the place where milk products are sold

domestic (dum ES tik)—tamed and raised by man

heifer (HEH fur)—young female cattle

polled (POLED)—cattle of hornless breed

steer (STEER)—male cattle which cannot father calves

udder (UH der)—a cow's milk sack

INDEX